The Wealth Equation

Understanding the Math Behind Money and Mind

— Ramesh Chauhan

ISBN: 9798301532795
Imprint: Independently published

Dedication

To my students, whose curiosity and drive inspire me every day.
To my readers, who seek knowledge not just to grow financially, but to grow as human beings. And to my family, for their unwavering support and belief in my vision.

Epigraph

"Wealth consists not in having great possessions, but in having few wants."
—Epictetus

Acknowledgments

This book is the result of countless conversations, reflections, and moments of learning. I am deeply grateful to:

- My students, whose questions and insights have shaped my understanding of the world.
- My readers, who continue to inspire me to write with purpose and clarity.
- My family and friends, who have supported me through every step of my teaching and writing journey.
- The mentors and authors whose works have profoundly influenced my thinking about wealth, life, and success.
  Thank you for being part of this journey.

Disclaimer

This book is intended for informational and educational purposes only. The strategies, examples, and ideas presented are based on the author's personal experiences and research. They are not a substitute for professional financial, legal, or investment advice. Readers should consult appropriate professionals to determine what is suitable for their individual circumstances. The author and publisher disclaim any liability for the outcomes of applying the information provided in this book.

Preface

The idea for this book was born from a realization I had over years of teaching and writing: that wealth is not just a number in a bank account but a state of mind. In my 30 years as a teacher and 15 years as a writer, I've seen people struggle with the same question: *How do I achieve true financial success?*

This book bridges two crucial aspects of wealth-building—the analytical and the psychological. While mastering budgets, investments, and interest is vital, understanding how your habits, emotions, and mindset influence your financial decisions is the key to lasting success.

The **RC Wealth Formula** is my way of simplifying and unifying these concepts into a framework that anyone can use. My hope is that this book will inspire you to not only manage your finances effectively but also cultivate a mindset that supports your goals, values, and dreams.

Prologue

Imagine two people starting their financial journey. One diligently calculates every expense, maximizes investments, and tracks market trends—but struggles with fear, impatience, and impulsive decisions. The other takes a modest, consistent approach, driven by a calm, disciplined mindset and a clear sense of purpose.

Who do you think builds wealth more effectively?

This book is about uncovering the missing piece in wealth-building: the alignment of math and mindset. By the time you finish reading, you'll have the tools to manage your money wisely and the mental strength to make decisions that support your long-term goals. Let's embark on this journey to decode **The Wealth Equation** together.

CONTENTS

Dedication 3
Epigraph 3
Acknowledgments 3
Preface 4
Prologue 5
Introduction: Decoding the Wealth Equation 19
   The Two Sides of the Wealth Equation 20
      1. The Math 20
      2. The Mind 20
   The Theme: Mastering Internal Variables for True Wealth 21
   What You'll Learn 21
   The Promise 22
Part 1: The Analytical Side – The Math of Money 25
Chapter 1: The Basics of the Wealth Equation 27
   The Five Core Components of Financial Math 27
      1. Income: The Starting Point of Your Wealth Equation 27
      2. Expenses: The Invisible Drain 28
      3. Savings: The Wealth You Keep 28
      4. Debt: The Opposite of Savings 28
      5. Investments: The Wealth Multiplier 29
   How the Components Interact 29
      The Wealth Equation 29
   Introducing Financial Leverage 30

    1. Increasing Income 30

    2. Reducing Expenses 30

    3. Eliminating Debt 31

    4. Consistently Saving and Investing 31

    A Simple Example of Financial Leverage in Action 31

    Key Takeaways 32

Chapter 2: Compound Interest – The Magic of Time 33

    The Math of Compound Interest 33

    The Power of Time in Action 34

        Example 1: Starting Early vs. Starting Late 34

        Key Insight: Starting early, even with smaller contributions, is more powerful than starting later with larger amounts. 35

    The Dark Side of Compound Interest: Debt 35

        Example 2: How Debt Compounds 35

        Key Insight: Compound interest doesn't discriminate—it works for or against you, depending on whether you're investing or borrowing. 35

    Why Time is Your Greatest Ally 35

    The Psychological Hurdle: Delayed Gratification . 36

        The Problem with Instant Rewards 36

        The Marshmallow Test and Money 37

    How to Overcome the Hurdle 37

        1. Visualize Your Future Self 37

        2. Automate Your Investments 37

        3. Start Small and Stay Consistent 38

Key Takeaways 38
Chapter 3: Budgets and Financial Systems 39
  The Math of Budgeting: A Simple Framework 39
    1. The 50/30/20 Rule 39
    2. Zero-Based Budgeting 40
  Building a Sustainable Budget 40
    1. Track Your Spending 41
    2. Prioritize Your Goals 41
    3. Build Flexibility 41
  The Psychology of Budgeting 41
    Why People Hate Budgets 42
    How to Make Budgeting Empowering 42
  The Role of Automation 42
    What to Automate 42
    The Benefits of Automation 43
    Example: The Automated Budget in Action 43
  Key Takeaways 44
Chapter 4: Investment Basics – Multiplying Your Wealth 45
  The Math of Investing: The Four Key Concepts 45
    1. Risk 45
    2. Return 46
    3. Diversification 46
    4. Time Horizons 46
  The Different Asset Classes 47
    1. Stocks 47
    2. Bonds 47

- 3. Real Estate 48
- 4. Mutual Funds and ETFs 48
- 5. Alternative Investments 48

Consistency and Long-Term Thinking: The Real Key to Wealth 49

- Dollar-Cost Averaging (DCA) 49
- The Power of Long-Term Thinking 49
- Example: The Long-Term Investor 50
- Key Takeaways 50

Part 2: The Psychological Side – The Mind Behind Money 53

Chapter 5: The Mental Variables in the Wealth Equation 55

- The Mental Variables That Shape Financial Success 55
- The RC Wealth Equation: Bridging Material and Mental Wealth 56
  - Breaking Down the Equation 56
- The Story Behind the RC Wealth Formula 57
- Key Implications of the Equation 57
  - Material Wealth Without Mental Wealth Falls Short 57
  - Mental Wealth Enhances Material Wealth 58
- Illustrative Scenarios 58
- Financial Behavior: Why Knowing the Math Isn't Enough 59
- Strengthening Your Mental Wealth Factor 59
- The Synergy Between Material and Mental Wealth 60

Chapter 6: Delayed Gratification – The Key to Unlocking Wealth 62
- **The Psychology of Delayed Gratification** 62
- **Lessons from the Marshmallow Test** 62
- **Why Delayed Gratification is Critical for Wealth** ... 63
- **Strategies to Build Delayed Gratification** 64
  - **1. Set Clear Financial Goals** 64
  - **2. Visualize Long-Term Benefits** 64
  - **3. Automate Financial Decisions** 64
  - **4. Create a Reward System** 64
  - **5. Practice Gradual Delays** 64
  - **6. Reframe Spending Temptations** 65
- **The Link Between Patience and Prosperity** 65
  - **Real-Life Example:** 65
- **Key Takeaways** 65

Chapter 7: The Emotional Costs of Wealth 67
- **The Hidden Emotional Costs of Wealth** 67
  - **1. Stress** 67
  - **2. Fear** 67
  - **3. Guilt** 68
  - **4. Comparison** 68
- **Emotional Spending and Lifestyle Inflation** 68
  - **1. The Trap of Emotional Spending** 68
  - **2. Lifestyle Inflation** 68
  - **3. The Underlying Cause: Emotional Triggers** ... 69
- **Overcoming FOMO and Detaching Self-Worth from Material Possessions** 69

1. Understanding FOMO 69
2. Shifting Your Mindset 69
3. Detaching Self-Worth from Material Possessions 70

Strategies to Navigate the Emotional Side of Money 70

1. Embrace Emotional Awareness 70
2. Set Emotional Boundaries 70
3. Create a Value-Based Budget 71
4. Practice Mindful Spending 71

Key Takeaways 71

Chapter 8: Building Wealth Habits That Last 73

The Psychology of Habit Formation 73

Why Habits Matter in Wealth-Building 73

The Power of Small, Consistent Actions 74

1. The $10/Day Principle 74
2. Regular Investments 74
3. Behavioral Compounding 74

Creating "Default Habits" for Wealth 75

1. Automate Good Financial Decisions 75
2. Attach Habits to Existing Routines 75
3. Use Visual Cues 76
4. Set SMART Goals 76
5. Leverage Rewards to Reinforce Habits 76

Overcoming Challenges in Habit Formation 77

1. Breaking Bad Habits 77
2. Staying Consistent 77

3. Adapting Over Time 77
A Life Built on Wealth Habits 77
Part 3: Solving the Wealth Equation – Aligning Math and Mind.. 79
   Chapter 9: The Long-Term Mindset – Thinking Like the Wealthy.. 81
      The Wealthy Mindset: How the Wealthy Think Differently 81
      Applying the RC Wealth Formula to the Long-Term Mindset.. 82
         How It Relates to Time, Risk, and Money:.......... 82
         The Role of Mental Wealth in Long-Term Thinking.. 82
      Focusing on Long-Term Goals 83
         Why Long-Term Goals Matter 83
         How to Stay Focused on the Long Term............ 83
      Reframing Your Mindset: From Instant Gratification to Financial Independence................ 84
      Real-Life Applications of the Long-Term Mindset 85
         Case Study 1: Early Investor............................... 85
         Case Study 2: Short-Term Thinker 85
      Strategies to Cultivate a Long-Term Mindset........ 85
         1. Visualize Your Future Self.............................. 85
         2. Adopt the "1% Rule" 85
         3. Avoid Emotional Decisions 86
         4. Surround Yourself with the Right Influences 86
      The Wealthy Think Long-Term—and So Can You 86

Chapter 10: The Power of Consistency and Incremental Gains 88
- The Role of Consistency in Wealth-Building.........88
  - Why Consistency Works..88
- The "1% Rule": Tiny Improvements with Massive Results 89
  - The Math of 1% Improvements...........................89
  - The Mindset of 1% Gains 89
- Avoiding the Trap of "Big Leaps" 89
  - The Risks of "Big Leaps" 90
  - The Alternative: Steady, Sustainable Growth....90
- Applying the RC Wealth Formula to Consistency 90
  - How Consistency Impacts the Formula: 90
- Strategies for Building Consistency 91
  - 1. Start Small and Scale Up 91
  - 2. Automate Your Finances 91
  - 3. Track Progress and Celebrate Wins...............91
  - 4. Focus on Long-Term Goals.............................91
  - 5. Embrace the Power of Routine 91
- Real-Life Examples of Incremental Gains 92
  - Case Study 1: The Steady Saver........................92
  - Case Study 2: The Big Leaper............................92
- Consistency: The Bridge Between Math and Mind 92
- Final Thoughts 93

Chapter 11: Financial Freedom Redefined...................94
- Redefining Financial Freedom...............................94

- Financial Freedom Is: 94
- Financial Freedom Is Not: 95
- The Concept of "Enough" 95
  - What Does "Enough" Mean? 95
  - The Pitfalls of Chasing More 95
  - How to Find Your "Enough" 96
- Aligning Financial Goals with Values and Purpose 97
  - Step 1: Reflect on Your Values 97
  - Step 2: Identify Your Life Purpose 97
  - Step 3: Set Purpose-Driven Goals 98
- A New Definition of Success 98
- The Ripple Effect of Financial Freedom 98
- Key Takeaways 99

Conclusion: Mastering the Wealth Equation 101
- Balancing the Math and the Mind 101
- Financial Success is About Alignment 102
  - What Alignment Looks Like: 102
- Approaching Your Finances with Confidence 102
- The Final Word: Wealth is More Than Numbers 102

Appendix and Bonus Material 105
- Appendix 1: Quick Reference Financial Tools 107
  - 1. Sample Budget Templates 107
    - The 50/30/20 Budget Template 107
    - Zero-Based Budget Template 109
  - 2. Compound Interest Calculator 110
    - Example 110

- Online Tools 110
- 3. Investment Tracking Spreadsheet 110

Appendix 2: Wealth Mindset Exercises 112
- **1. Journaling Prompts to Reframe Money Beliefs** 112
- **2. Visualization Exercise for Long-Term Goals** ... 112
  - Step 1: Imagine Your Future Self 112
  - Step 2: Write It Down 113
  - Step 3: Break It Into Steps 113
- **3. Habit-Tracking Templates** 114

Appendix 3: Recommended Reading and Resources 115
- Books 115
- Podcasts 115
- Online Tools 115

Appendix 4: The RC Wealth Equation – Bridging Material and Mental Wealth 117
- **The RC Wealth Equation** 117
- **Breaking Down the Equation** 117
  - 1. Material Wealth 117
  - 2. Mental Wealth Factor 118
- **What the Equation Teaches Us** 118
  - Key Implications of the Equation 118
- **Illustrative Scenarios** 119
  - Scenario 1: High Material Wealth, Low Mental Wealth 119
  - Scenario 2: Moderate Material Wealth, High Mental Wealth 120

How to Increase Your Mental Wealth Factor 120

The Synergy of Math and Mindset 121

Practical Steps to Apply the RC Wealth Equation
.... 121

Final Note: Unlocking Real Wealth 122

Introduction: Decoding the Wealth Equation

When most people think about building wealth, they picture numbers. They imagine spreadsheets filled with budgets, calculators crunching compound interest, and stock market charts tracking investments. They believe financial success is all about mastering the math—getting the formulas right, optimizing returns, and eliminating debt. And while the math is undeniably important, it's only one part of the equation.

The truth is, financial success isn't just about numbers. If it were, we'd all be wealthy, because the numbers are accessible to everyone. The formulas for compounding wealth, saving money, and investing wisely are universal and relatively simple to understand. So why do so many people struggle to achieve financial freedom?

The answer lies in the other side of the wealth equation: the *mind*.

We don't make financial decisions in a vacuum. Every choice we make is influenced by our emotions, habits, fears, and beliefs about money. Why do we overspend when we know we should save? Why do we hesitate to invest even when the numbers tell us it's the smartest move? Why do we abandon long-term goals for short-term gratification?

The wealth equation isn't just about budgets and interest rates—it's about how we think and feel about money. True wealth is built when we combine the analytical side of finance (the math) with the psychological side (the mind).

The Two Sides of the Wealth Equation

1. The Math

The math side of the wealth equation is where most financial advice begins—and ends. It includes the tangible, logical aspects of managing money, like:

- Understanding how to budget your income and track expenses.
- Knowing how to calculate interest rates and leverage compound growth.
- Investing in diverse assets to build wealth over time.

These are essential skills, and mastering them gives you the foundation for financial success. But math alone doesn't guarantee results. Even the most well-designed budget can fall apart if it's not paired with the discipline to follow it. A perfectly optimized investment plan won't work if fear keeps you from taking action.

2. The Mind

The mind side of the wealth equation is where the true challenge lies. This is where emotions, habits, and beliefs influence how we handle money. Key psychological variables include:

- **Patience**: Can you delay gratification today to achieve greater rewards tomorrow?
- **Consistency**: Are you able to stick with a plan, even when progress feels slow?
- **Emotions**: Can you manage fear, greed, and impulsivity when making financial decisions?
- **Habits**: Do your daily routines support your financial goals, or do they sabotage them?

Unlike the math, which is universal, the mind side of the equation is deeply personal. Everyone has their own mental "wealth equation," shaped by experiences, upbringing, and beliefs. And if the mental variables aren't in alignment, no amount of math will lead to lasting financial success.

The Theme: Mastering Internal Variables for True Wealth

True wealth isn't just built by solving for X on a spreadsheet. It's built by solving for the hidden variables within yourself.

Consider this: Two people with the same income, expenses, and investment strategy can end up in drastically different financial situations. Why? Because one person might have the patience to let their investments grow, while the other might pull out at the first sign of market volatility. One might have the discipline to stick to their budget, while the other might give in to emotional spending.

The difference isn't in the math—it's in the mind.

This book is about mastering both sides of the wealth equation. It's about teaching you the numbers while also helping you build the mindset that will allow you to apply those numbers effectively. Because when you align your internal variables—your patience, habits, and emotional intelligence—with sound financial principles, that's when wealth truly begins to grow.

What You'll Learn

This book will show you how to balance the two sides of the wealth equation to create a life of financial freedom and security. Together, we'll explore:

- The **analytical side**: You'll learn the foundational math of wealth, including budgeting, compounding, and investing. These tools will give you the knowledge to make informed decisions about your money.
- The **psychological side**: You'll uncover the hidden mental variables that impact your financial behavior. You'll learn how to manage fear, build consistency, and develop habits that align with your long-term goals.

This isn't a book about complicated financial formulas or advanced investing strategies. Instead, it's a guide to understanding how the numbers and your mindset work together—and how mastering both will unlock your potential for wealth-building.

The Promise

By the end of this book, you won't just understand the math behind money—you'll understand yourself. You'll gain practical tools to improve your financial situation and psychological strategies to overcome the emotional and mental barriers that have held you back.

Whether you're trying to pay off debt, save for a big goal, or build a nest egg for the future, this book will give you the clarity and confidence to take control of your financial destiny.

Remember: The wealth equation isn't just about what you have—it's about who you become in the process. You already have everything you need to succeed. This book will show you how to unlock it.

Let's get started. Your journey to mastering the wealth equation begins now.

Part 1: The Analytical Side – The Math of Money

Chapter 1: The Basics of the Wealth Equation

At its core, money is math. Every financial decision—whether it's budgeting, paying off debt, or investing—is built on simple equations that govern how money flows into and out of your life. While these equations may seem basic on the surface, the way you use them can have a profound impact on your financial future.

This chapter lays the foundation by defining the key components of financial math and showing how small, intentional changes can dramatically shift your wealth-building trajectory over time. You don't need to be a mathematician to master this side of the wealth equation—you just need to understand how the numbers interact and what they mean for your financial life.

The Five Core Components of Financial Math

Think of your finances as a system with five interconnected components:

1. **Income**: The money you earn.
2. **Expenses**: The money you spend.
3. **Savings**: The money you keep.
4. **Debt**: The money you owe.
5. **Investments**: The money you grow.

Let's take a closer look at each component:

1. Income: The Starting Point of Your Wealth Equation

Income is the foundation of your financial system. It includes all sources of money flowing into your life—your salary, side hustles, rental income, dividends, or other earnings. While income is often seen as the primary driver of wealth, it's important to remember that income alone doesn't build wealth. What you do with your income is what matters.

2. Expenses: The Invisible Drain

Expenses are the money flowing out of your life to cover your needs and wants. They include essentials (housing, food, transportation) and non-essentials (entertainment, shopping, subscriptions). Expenses directly impact how much money you have left to save or invest.

3. Savings: The Wealth You Keep

Savings are what's left after you subtract your expenses from your income. The formula is simple:

Income - Expenses = Savings

However, savings don't grow by themselves—they need to be actively nurtured. While it's tempting to spend all the money you earn, consistently saving is what lays the groundwork for building long-term wealth.

4. Debt: The Opposite of Savings

Debt is money you've borrowed that must be repaid, often with interest. While some debt (like a mortgage or student loans) can be considered an investment in your future, high-interest consumer debt (like credit cards) can quickly derail your financial progress.

Debt creates a negative drag on your wealth equation: **Income - (Expenses + Debt Payments) = Savings**

Paying down debt reduces that drag, freeing up more of your money to save and invest.

5. Investments: The Wealth Multiplier

Investments are where your money works for you. By putting your money into assets like stocks, bonds, real estate, or businesses, you give it the opportunity to grow through compound interest, dividends, or appreciation. Investments are the key to turning savings into long-term wealth.

How the Components Interact

Each of these components is part of a larger system, and small changes in one can have a ripple effect across the entire equation. Let's break it down:

The Wealth Equation

At its simplest, the wealth equation looks like this:

Income - Expenses = Savings

But as you start to save and invest, it evolves:

(Income - Expenses - Debt Payments) + Investment Growth = Wealth

Each variable plays a role:

- **Increasing income** gives you more money to save, invest, or pay off debt.
- **Reducing expenses** frees up money for savings or investments.
- **Eliminating debt** reduces the drag on your financial progress.

- **Investing consistently** grows your wealth exponentially over time.

Introducing Financial Leverage

Small changes in any one variable—income, expenses, savings, debt, or investments—can lead to outsized results over time. This concept is known as **financial leverage**: maximizing the impact of your efforts by strategically adjusting the variables in your wealth equation.

1. Increasing Income

Let's say you find a way to increase your income by $500 per month, whether through a raise, side hustle, or freelance work. That $500 can be directed toward:

- Paying off debt faster.
- Boosting your savings rate.
- Investing to grow your wealth.

Even small increases in income, when directed wisely, can accelerate your financial progress.

2. Reducing Expenses

Reducing expenses is often one of the most immediate ways to improve your wealth equation. For example:

- Cutting $200 a month by eating out less saves $2,400 a year.
- Canceling unused subscriptions could free up an extra $50 a month.

The key is directing these savings toward debt repayment, emergency funds, or investments rather than letting them disappear into other expenses.

3. Eliminating Debt

Debt repayment has a compounding effect on your wealth equation. For example:

- Paying off a credit card with a 20% interest rate is like earning a 20% return on your money.
- Once debt is eliminated, you can redirect those payments toward savings or investments.

Debt is like running a race with a weight tied to your ankle—eliminating it makes every step forward easier.

4. Consistently Saving and Investing

Consistency is where financial leverage truly shines. By saving and investing regularly—even small amounts—you allow compound interest to work in your favor. For example:

- Saving $100 per month at a 7% annual return grows to $12,409 in 10 years.
- Saving $500 per month grows to $62,046 in the same timeframe.

The earlier you start and the more consistent you are, the greater your results.

A Simple Example of Financial Leverage in Action

Let's imagine two individuals, Alice and Bob, who earn the same income.

- **Alice:** Spends most of her income, saves inconsistently, and has high-interest credit card debt.

- **Bob:** Reduces unnecessary expenses, saves 20% of his income, and invests consistently.

After 10 years:

- Alice's high expenses and interest payments have kept her wealth stagnant.
- Bob, thanks to financial leverage (cutting expenses, investing savings, and eliminating debt), has built significant wealth.

The math was the same for both—what changed was how they used the variables.

Key Takeaways

- **The math of money is simple, but its application is powerful.** Understanding how income, expenses, savings, debt, and investments interact is the first step to building wealth.
- **Small changes can lead to big results.** Increasing income, reducing expenses, eliminating debt, and investing consistently all create financial leverage that accelerates your progress.
- **The key to wealth-building is intentionality.** Each financial decision you make impacts the equation—choose wisely.

In the next chapter, we'll explore one of the most powerful forces in the wealth equation: compound interest. You'll see how time can amplify your efforts and turn even small investments into significant long-term gains.

Let's move forward—your wealth equation is waiting to be optimized.

Chapter 2: Compound Interest – The Magic of Time

Albert Einstein is often credited with calling compound interest the "eighth wonder of the world," saying, *"He who understands it, earns it; he who doesn't, pays it."* While it may sound like an exaggeration, there's a reason why this simple mathematical concept is considered one of the most powerful forces in building wealth.

Compound interest is the process by which your money grows not only on your initial investment but also on the interest it earns. Over time, this compounding effect can turn even small, consistent contributions into a significant fortune. However, this same force can also work against you when it comes to debt.

In this chapter, we'll explore the math of compound interest, how time is its greatest ally (or enemy), and why the psychology of delayed gratification often prevents people from harnessing its full power.

The Math of Compound Interest

At its core, compound interest is interest earning interest. Instead of only growing your principal investment, compound interest allows the growth to accelerate exponentially as time goes on.

The formula for compound interest is:

$A = P(1 + r/n)^{(nt)}$
Where:

- **A** = the future value of the investment or loan, including interest

- **P** = the principal (initial amount of money)
- **r** = the annual interest rate (decimal form, e.g., 0.05 for 5%)
- **n** = the number of times interest is compounded per year
- **t** = the time the money is invested or borrowed, in years

At first glance, this formula might seem complicated, but its real power lies in one simple factor: **time**. The longer your money has to grow, the more dramatic the compounding effect becomes.

The Power of Time in Action

Let's look at an example to see how compound interest works in practice:

Example 1: Starting Early vs. Starting Late

Imagine two people, Emma and Jack:

- **Emma** starts investing $5,000 per year at age 25 and stops contributing at age 35 (10 years total).
- **Jack** starts investing $5,000 per year at age 35 and continues until age 65 (30 years total).

Both earn an annual return of 7%. Here's what happens:

- By age 65, Emma's investment grows to **$602,070**, even though she only invested $50,000 over 10 years.
- Jack's investment grows to **$540,741**, even though he invested $150,000 over 30 years.

Why did Emma end up with more money, even though she contributed far less? The answer is **time**. Her early start allowed compound interest to work its magic for 40 years, while Jack's money only compounded for 30 years.

Key Insight: Starting early, even with smaller contributions, is more powerful than starting later with larger amounts.

The Dark Side of Compound Interest: Debt

The same force that builds wealth can also amplify debt. When you carry high-interest debt, like credit card balances or payday loans, compound interest works against you, growing the amount you owe exponentially.

Example 2: How Debt Compounds

Let's say you have $10,000 in credit card debt with a 20% annual interest rate, and you make no payments. Using the same formula, here's how your debt grows:

- After 1 year: $12,000
- After 5 years: $24,883
- After 10 years: $61,917

That initial $10,000 debt balloons into over $60,000 in just 10 years—without you borrowing a single additional dollar.

Key Insight: Compound interest doesn't discriminate—it works for or against you, depending on whether you're investing or borrowing.

Why Time is Your Greatest Ally

Compound interest is most powerful when paired with time. The longer your money has to grow, the more significant the compounding effect becomes.

Here's why:

- **Exponential Growth**: In the early years, your money grows slowly, but over time, the growth accelerates dramatically. This is why compound interest is often compared to a snowball rolling downhill—it starts small but grows larger and faster as it picks up momentum.
- **"The Rule of 72"**: This simple rule helps estimate how long it will take for an investment to double, given a fixed annual return. Divide 72 by your interest rate:
    - At 6%, your money doubles in 12 years.
    - At 8%, it doubles in 9 years.

The earlier you start investing, the more doubling cycles you can achieve, which is why time is your most valuable asset.

The Psychological Hurdle: Delayed Gratification

If compound interest is so powerful, why don't more people take full advantage of it? The answer lies in the psychological challenge of **delayed gratification**.

The Problem with Instant Rewards

Humans are hardwired to prioritize immediate rewards over long-term benefits. This is known as *present bias*. It's why we choose to:

- Spend money on things we don't need today instead of saving for tomorrow.
- Avoid investing because we don't see immediate results.

Compound interest rewards patience, but most people struggle to wait long enough to see its effects.

The Marshmallow Test and Money

The famous Marshmallow Test, conducted by psychologist Walter Mischel, demonstrated that children who could delay gratification (waiting for two marshmallows instead of eating one right away) were more likely to succeed later in life. The same principle applies to wealth-building:

- Those who can delay gratification (saving and investing instead of spending impulsively) are more likely to achieve financial success.

How to Overcome the Hurdle

1. Visualize Your Future Self

It's hard to save for "future you" if you don't feel connected to them. Take a moment to imagine your future self at retirement:

- What kind of life do you want to live?
- How will today's decisions impact that version of yourself?

Reminding yourself of your long-term goals can make it easier to prioritize saving and investing over short-term spending.

2. Automate Your Investments

One way to bypass the temptation to spend is to automate your savings and investments. Set up automatic transfers to your savings or investment accounts so you never see the money in your checking account.

3. Start Small and Stay Consistent

Even small contributions add up over time. If saving $500 a month feels overwhelming, start with $50 and gradually increase as your income grows. The key is consistency—small amounts invested regularly grow into significant wealth over time.

Key Takeaways

1. **Compound interest is the most powerful tool in wealth-building.** The longer you let your money grow, the more dramatic the results.
2. **Time is your greatest ally or enemy.** Start investing as early as possible to harness the full power of compounding—and avoid letting debt grow unchecked.
3. **Patience is the price of admission.** Delayed gratification is essential to building wealth, but automation and visualization can help make it easier.

In the next chapter, we'll take these insights a step further by exploring practical strategies for creating a budget and building a financial system that supports consistent saving and investing. Because understanding compound interest is just the beginning—what you do with it is what truly matters.

Let's keep building. Your wealth equation is just getting started.

Chapter 3: Budgets and Financial Systems

Budgeting often gets a bad reputation. For many people, the word "budget" feels restrictive, like a financial straitjacket that limits freedom and enjoyment. But in reality, a good budget is the opposite—it's a tool for empowerment. A well-designed budget doesn't control your life; it gives you clarity and control over your money, allowing you to prioritize what truly matters while building long-term wealth.

In this chapter, we'll break down the math of creating a sustainable budget, explore the psychology of budgeting (and why most people avoid it), and introduce automation as a powerful strategy to make budgeting easier and more effective.

The Math of Budgeting: A Simple Framework

At its core, budgeting is about creating a plan for how you'll allocate your income across three key areas:

1. **Needs**: Essential expenses like housing, utilities, food, and transportation.
2. **Wants**: Non-essential expenses that enhance your quality of life, like dining out, entertainment, or hobbies.
3. **Savings/Investments**: The money you set aside for the future, including emergency funds, retirement, and wealth-building.

Two popular budgeting methods help simplify this process:

1. The 50/30/20 Rule

The 50/30/20 rule provides a general guideline for allocating your income:

- **50% for Needs**: Rent, groceries, insurance, utilities, etc.
- **30% for Wants**: Entertainment, vacations, subscriptions, dining out, etc.
- **20% for Savings/Investments**: Emergency funds, retirement accounts, paying off debt, etc.

This rule works well as a starting point for people who want simplicity. However, your percentages may vary depending on your financial goals or life circumstances. For example, if you're aggressively paying off debt or saving for a big purchase, you might adjust to 50/20/30 (with 30% going to savings).

2. Zero-Based Budgeting

Zero-based budgeting ensures that every dollar of your income has a purpose. The formula is simple:

Income - Expenses = $0

Here's how it works:

1. List your total monthly income.
2. Assign every dollar to a specific category, such as rent, groceries, savings, or entertainment, until your income minus expenses equals zero.
3. Adjust as needed to make sure your priorities (like savings or debt repayment) are funded first.

Zero-based budgeting is ideal for people who want maximum control and transparency over their finances.

Building a Sustainable Budget

A sustainable budget is one you can stick to long-term. Here are some practical tips to make it work:

1. Track Your Spending

Before creating a budget, it's essential to understand where your money is currently going. Use a tool like a spreadsheet, budgeting app, or even pen and paper to track every expense for a month. This will give you a clear picture of your spending habits and help you identify areas where you can cut back.

2. Prioritize Your Goals

Budgets are most effective when they're aligned with your financial goals. Ask yourself:

- What do I want to achieve with my money? (e.g., pay off debt, save for a home, retire early)
- How can I adjust my spending to make progress toward these goals?

3. Build Flexibility

Life is unpredictable, and a rigid budget can feel discouraging if it doesn't account for unexpected expenses or moments of indulgence. Leave some wiggle room in your budget to accommodate surprises without feeling like you've "failed."

The Psychology of Budgeting

While the math of budgeting is straightforward, the emotions tied to money can make it challenging to stick to a plan. Here's why many people hate budgets—and how to reframe them as empowering instead of restrictive:

Why People Hate Budgets

1. **Budgets Feel Restrictive**: People associate budgets with sacrifice and deprivation.
2. **Fear of Confronting Reality**: Tracking expenses can reveal overspending or financial mistakes, which can feel overwhelming.
3. **Lack of Motivation**: Without a clear goal, budgeting can feel like an exercise in discipline without a purpose.

How to Make Budgeting Empowering

1. **Reframe Your Mindset**: Instead of thinking of a budget as a restriction, see it as a tool for freedom. A budget allows you to spend guilt-free on things that matter while cutting out expenses that don't align with your values.
2. **Focus on Your "Why"**: Tie your budget to a meaningful goal. For example, saving for a dream vacation or building an emergency fund for peace of mind can make the process feel rewarding.
3. **Celebrate Progress**: Track your wins—whether it's paying off a credit card, hitting a savings milestone, or reducing unnecessary spending—and reward yourself in small, meaningful ways.

The Role of Automation

Automation removes the emotional decision-making from your finances, making it easier to stick to your budget and reach your goals without constant effort. By setting up systems that run in the background, you can ensure your money is working for you.

What to Automate

1. **Savings**: Set up automatic transfers to your savings account on payday. This "pay yourself first" approach ensures you save before spending.
2. **Debt Payments**: Automate minimum payments or extra payments on loans to avoid missed deadlines and reduce interest.
3. **Investments**: Use automatic contributions to retirement accounts (401(k), IRA) or investment accounts to build wealth consistently over time.
4. **Recurring Bills**: Automate payments for utilities, insurance, and subscriptions to avoid late fees and free up mental energy.

The Benefits of Automation

- **Consistency**: Ensures you save, invest, or pay down debt every month without fail.
- **Eliminates Temptation**: Removes the temptation to spend money earmarked for savings or investments.
- **Reduces Stress**: Frees you from worrying about deadlines or forgetting to move money manually.

Example: The Automated Budget in Action

Imagine you earn $4,000 per month and use automation to create a hands-off budget:

- $800 (20%) is automatically transferred to your savings and investment accounts.
- $1,600 (40%) is automated for rent and utilities.
- $600 (15%) is allocated to recurring debt payments.
- The remaining $1,000 (25%) is left for discretionary spending, split across categories like groceries, entertainment, and dining out.

With this system, your financial priorities are handled automatically, and you're free to enjoy your discretionary money without guilt or second-guessing.

Key Takeaways

1. **Budgeting is a tool for empowerment, not restriction.** A sustainable budget aligns with your goals and values, giving you clarity and control over your finances.
2. **Simple frameworks like the 50/30/20 rule and zero-based budgeting can help you allocate your income effectively.**
3. **Automation is your secret weapon.** By automating savings, investments, and payments, you can remove emotion from financial decisions and ensure consistent progress.
4. **The psychology of budgeting matters.** When you focus on your "why" and celebrate progress, budgeting becomes a rewarding practice instead of a chore.

In the next chapter, we'll dive into the basics of investing—where your money doesn't just sit but grows and multiplies. Because while budgeting is about controlling your income, investing is about unlocking its full potential.

Let's keep building your financial system—one intentional step at a time.

Chapter 4: Investment Basics – Multiplying Your Wealth

Budgeting and saving are the foundation of financial success, but wealth isn't built by simply putting money aside—it's built by making your money work for you. That's where investing comes in.

Investing is often perceived as complex and intimidating, but at its core, it's a simple concept: you put your money into assets that have the potential to grow over time. Through the power of compounding, those assets generate returns that multiply your wealth far beyond what's possible with savings alone.

In this chapter, we'll simplify the math of investing, introduce you to different types of investment options, and explain how consistent, long-term investing can transform your financial future.

The Math of Investing: The Four Key Concepts

To understand investing, you only need to grasp four basic concepts:

1. Risk

Risk is the potential for your investment to lose value. Every type of investment carries some level of risk, but higher risks often come with higher potential rewards.

- Low-risk investments (like bonds) are less likely to lose value but often provide lower returns.
- High-risk investments (like stocks) have more volatility but offer the potential for greater gains over time.

2. Return

Return is the profit you earn from your investment. This can come in different forms:

- **Capital Gains**: The increase in the value of an asset (e.g., you buy a stock for $50, and it grows to $100).
- **Dividends or Interest**: Payments you receive from your investments, such as dividends from stocks or interest from bonds.

Returns are typically expressed as a percentage of your initial investment. For example, if you invest $1,000 and earn a 10% return, your profit is $100.

3. Diversification

Diversification is the practice of spreading your investments across different types of assets to reduce risk. The idea is simple: don't put all your eggs in one basket.

- For example, if you invest all your money in one company's stock and that company fails, you could lose everything. But if you spread your investments across multiple companies, industries, or asset classes, a loss in one area can be offset by gains in another.

4. Time Horizons

Your time horizon is the length of time you plan to hold an investment before you need the money.

- **Short-Term Horizon**: Less than 3 years (e.g., saving for a vacation). Short-term investments should prioritize stability over growth.

- **Long-Term Horizon**: 10+ years (e.g., retirement). Long-term investments can handle more risk because they have time to recover from market fluctuations.

The longer your time horizon, the more you can benefit from the compounding growth of your investments.

The Different Asset Classes

Investing isn't a one-size-fits-all approach. There are several asset classes to choose from, each with its own characteristics, risks, and potential returns. Understanding these options is key to building a diversified investment portfolio.

1. Stocks

- **What They Are**: Stocks represent ownership in a company. When you buy a stock, you're purchasing a small piece of that company.
- **How They Work**: Stocks generate returns through capital gains (when the stock price increases) and dividends (periodic payments to shareholders).
- **Risk/Return**: Stocks are higher-risk but historically offer the highest long-term returns, averaging about 7–10% annually.

2. Bonds

- **What They Are**: Bonds are essentially loans you give to a company or government. In return, they pay you interest over a set period and return your principal at maturity.
- **How They Work**: Bonds generate returns through interest payments (also called coupon payments).

- **Risk/Return**: Bonds are lower-risk than stocks but also provide lower returns, averaging about 3–5% annually.

3. Real Estate

- **What It Is**: Real estate investing involves buying property to generate rental income or capital appreciation.
- **How It Works**: You can invest in physical properties (like rental homes) or indirectly through real estate investment trusts (REITs), which pool investor money to buy property portfolios.
- **Risk/Return**: Real estate offers moderate-to-high returns but comes with risks like market fluctuations, property management challenges, and illiquidity (difficulty selling quickly).

4. Mutual Funds and ETFs

- **What They Are**: Mutual funds and exchange-traded funds (ETFs) pool money from multiple investors to buy a diversified mix of stocks, bonds, or other assets.
- **How They Work**: You invest in the fund, and a professional manager or index determines its holdings. ETFs trade like stocks, while mutual funds are bought directly from the fund company.
- **Risk/Return**: Risk depends on the underlying assets, but these funds make diversification easy and are ideal for beginner investors.

5. Alternative Investments

- **What They Are**: These include commodities (like gold or oil), cryptocurrencies, collectibles, and private equity.

- **How They Work**: Alternative investments often behave differently from traditional assets, offering diversification benefits but higher risks.
- **Risk/Return**: Returns and risks vary widely. These are generally suited for more experienced investors.

Consistency and Long-Term Thinking: The Real Key to Wealth

One of the biggest mistakes people make with investing is trying to "time the market"—buying and selling assets based on short-term predictions. This approach is risky, stressful, and often unsuccessful. Instead, focus on consistency and long-term thinking.

Dollar-Cost Averaging (DCA)

Dollar-cost averaging involves investing a fixed amount of money at regular intervals, regardless of market conditions.

- **Example**: You invest $200 in the stock market every month, whether prices are up or down. Over time, this strategy reduces the impact of market volatility by buying more shares when prices are low and fewer when prices are high.
- **Why It Works**: DCA removes emotion from investing and ensures consistent contributions to your portfolio.

The Power of Long-Term Thinking

Investing isn't about quick wins; it's about playing the long game. Here's why:

1. **Time Smooths Volatility**: Over short periods, markets can be unpredictable, but over decades, they tend to trend upward.

2. **Compounding Growth**: As discussed in Chapter 2, the longer your money stays invested, the more time it has to grow exponentially.
3. **Avoid Emotional Decisions**: Long-term thinking helps you resist the urge to panic during market downturns, allowing you to stay invested and reap the rewards of recovery.

Example: The Long-Term Investor

Imagine you invest $500 a month in an index fund that earns an average annual return of 8%. Here's how your money grows over time:

- After 10 years: $91,473
- After 20 years: $247,115
- After 30 years: $593,053

The key? Consistency and time. By sticking to a simple plan, you can build significant wealth without needing to outsmart the market.

Key Takeaways

1. **Understand the math of investing.** Risk, return, diversification, and time horizons are the building blocks of smart investing.
2. **Diversify your portfolio.** Spreading your investments across asset classes like stocks, bonds, and real estate reduces risk while maximizing potential returns.
3. **Consistency is more important than timing.** Dollar-cost averaging and long-term thinking eliminate the need to predict market movements.

4. **Time is your best friend.** The longer you stay invested, the greater the impact of compounding growth on your wealth.

In the next chapter, we'll shift gears to explore the hidden mental and emotional variables that influence investing. Because while understanding the math is essential, managing your mindset is what ensures you stay consistent and confident over the long haul.

Let's move forward—your wealth is waiting to grow.

Part 2: The Psychological Side – The Mind Behind Money

Chapter 5: The Mental Variables in the Wealth Equation

When it comes to building wealth, most people focus on the numbers—income, savings, investments, and interest rates. While these factors are undeniably important, they only tell part of the story. Real financial success is about more than math; it's about mastering the psychological and emotional forces that influence how we handle money.

In this chapter, we'll uncover the hidden mental variables that drive your financial behavior, explore how biases and emotions can sabotage even the best financial plans, and introduce the concept of the Wealth Equation—a framework that shows how material wealth and mental wealth work together to create true financial success.

The Mental Variables That Shape Financial Success

While the analytical side of the wealth equation focuses on measurable elements like income and expenses, the mental side involves intangible variables that are just as important:

1. **Patience**
   Building wealth takes time, but in a world of instant gratification, patience is increasingly rare. Whether it's waiting for your investments to grow or resisting the urge to overspend, patience is the foundation of long-term success.
2. **Discipline**
   Discipline is the ability to stick to your financial plan, even when it's inconvenient or emotionally

challenging. It's saying no to short-term temptations so you can say yes to long-term goals.

3. **Emotional Intelligence**
Your ability to manage emotions like fear, greed, and frustration plays a huge role in financial decision-making. For example, panic during a market downturn or impulsive spending during stressful times can derail your progress.

4. **Mindset**
How you think about money—your beliefs, attitudes, and mental framework—shapes every financial decision you make. A scarcity mindset can make you cling to money out of fear, while an abundance mindset can help you take calculated risks to grow your wealth.

These mental variables aren't fixed—they can be developed and strengthened through self-awareness and intentional practice.

The RC Wealth Equation: Bridging Material and Mental Wealth

To understand the relationship between the math and the mind, let's consider the Wealth Equation:

Real Wealth=Material Wealth×(1+Mental Wealth Factor)

Breaking Down the Equation

- **Material Wealth**: This represents the tangible side of wealth—your income, savings, investments, and assets. It's what can be measured and calculated.
- **Mental Wealth Factor**: This is the multiplier that reflects your psychological alignment with money. It

includes variables like discipline, patience, emotional intelligence, and mindset.

The equation shows that material wealth alone doesn't define real wealth. Instead, real wealth is amplified (or diminished) by your mental wealth.

The Story Behind the RC Wealth Formula

When I think about real wealth, I see it as more than just financial assets. To me, true wealth is the result of a harmonious relationship between **Material Wealth** and **Mental Wealth**. This understanding led me to develop the **RC Wealth Formula**, named after my initials, Ramesh Chauhan.

The RC Wealth Formula captures the essence of how these two elements—math and mindset—work together:

Real Wealth = Material Wealth × (1 + Mental Wealth Factor)

This formula expresses my belief that material wealth is only as powerful as the mindset and habits that support it. A person with millions in the bank but poor financial habits may still struggle, while someone with modest income and a strong mental wealth factor can achieve incredible financial security and fulfillment.

The "RC" in the name represents my journey and perspective on this topic. Through this framework, I aim to show how anyone can amplify their wealth by strengthening the mental variables that often go unnoticed but are crucial for long-term success.

Key Implications of the Equation

Material Wealth Without Mental Wealth Falls Short

Even if you have substantial material wealth, a low Mental Wealth Factor (e.g., poor discipline, emotional spending) limits your ability to fully utilize and enjoy it.

Mental Wealth Enhances Material Wealth

When you have strong financial habits and emotional control, you maximize the impact of your material wealth. Even modest material wealth can feel significant when paired with a high Mental Wealth Factor.

Illustrative Scenarios

1. **High Material Wealth, Low Mental Wealth**
   - Material Wealth: $1,000,000
   - Mental Wealth Factor: 0.2 (minimal alignment, poor financial habits)
   - Real Wealth: $1,000,000 × (1 + 0.2) = $1,200,000
2. Even with high material wealth, the low Mental Wealth Factor only adds a modest boost. Emotional spending or impulsive financial decisions might cause this wealth to deplete quickly, leading to stress despite the large bank balance.
3. **Moderate Material Wealth, High Mental Wealth**
   - Material Wealth: $500,000
   - Mental Wealth Factor: 1.0 (strong financial habits and discipline)
   - Real Wealth: $500,000 × (1 + 1.0) = $1,000,000
4. Here, strong mental wealth doubles the effective Real Wealth. With disciplined spending, consistent investing, and emotional control, this individual feels financially secure and fulfilled, even with a smaller material base.

Financial Behavior: Why Knowing the Math Isn't Enough

Most people fail to build wealth not because they lack financial knowledge, but because they can't manage their financial behavior. Here's why:

1. **Emotional Decisions**
   Money is deeply tied to emotions like fear, greed, guilt, and pride. These emotions often lead to poor decisions, such as:
   - Selling investments during a market dip out of fear.
   - Overspending on luxuries to impress others.
   - Avoiding financial planning because it feels overwhelming or shameful.
2. **Biases That Sabotage Wealth**
   Human psychology is full of cognitive biases that distort our financial decisions. Let's explore a few:
   - **Loss Aversion**: The pain of losing money feels stronger than the joy of gaining it, which can lead to overly cautious behavior.
   - **Overconfidence**: Overestimating your ability to "beat the market" can lead to risky investments or lack of diversification.
   - **Herd Mentality**: Following what others are doing—whether it's panic-selling during a downturn or chasing a "hot" investment—often results in poor timing and missed opportunities.

Strengthening Your Mental Wealth Factor

The good news is that your Mental Wealth Factor is within your control. By cultivating patience, discipline, emotional intelligence, and a growth mindset, you can amplify the impact of your Material Wealth.

1. **Practice Patience**
   - Focus on long-term goals rather than short-term gains.
   - Remind yourself of the compounding effect of consistency over time.
2. **Build Discipline**
   - Automate savings and investments to reduce the temptation to overspend.
   - Create a budget that aligns with your values and stick to it.
3. **Develop Emotional Intelligence**
   - Practice mindfulness to observe your emotions without acting on them impulsively.
   - Reflect on financial decisions before making them—don't let fear or greed dictate your choices.
4. **Shift Your Mindset**
   - Replace a scarcity mindset with an abundance mindset.
   - Celebrate progress, even small wins, to stay motivated.

The Synergy Between Material and Mental Wealth

The RC Wealth Formula highlights an essential truth: True financial success isn't just about accumulating money; it's about managing it wisely and aligning it with your values and goals.

If your Mental Wealth Factor is high, even modest material wealth can provide a sense of security, fulfillment, and freedom.

If your Mental Wealth Factor is low, even significant material wealth may feel unstable or insufficient, leading to stress and dissatisfaction.

By improving your Mental Wealth Factor, you unlock the full potential of your Material Wealth and create a balanced, sustainable path to real financial success.

Chapter 6: Delayed Gratification – The Key to Unlocking Wealth

Building wealth requires more than just financial acumen; it demands mastery of the often-overlooked skill of **delayed gratification**. This chapter explores the psychology behind delayed gratification, its critical role in saving and investing, and actionable strategies to cultivate this essential habit.

The Psychology of Delayed Gratification

At its core, delayed gratification is the ability to resist the temptation of immediate rewards in favor of larger, long-term benefits. This concept is central to wealth-building because financial success rarely happens overnight—it's the result of small, consistent efforts compounded over time.

- **Immediate vs. Long-Term Rewards**:
    - *Immediate*: Spending money on non-essential luxuries.
    - *Long-Term*: Investing that money and watching it grow exponentially.

While the former provides instant satisfaction, the latter leads to sustained financial security and freedom. The challenge? Our brains are wired for immediate pleasure, making it difficult to resist short-term temptations.

Lessons from the Marshmallow Test

One of the most famous studies on delayed gratification is the **Stanford Marshmallow Experiment**. In this study, children were offered a choice: one marshmallow immediately or two marshmallows if they waited 15 minutes.

Key findings:

- Children who were able to wait (delayed gratification) tended to have better life outcomes, including higher academic achievement, better health, and greater financial stability.
- The ability to delay gratification wasn't innate but could be developed with practice.

What does this mean for wealth-building? The same principles apply. Those who can delay spending for future growth—through saving and investing—are more likely to achieve long-term financial success.

Why Delayed Gratification is Critical for Wealth

1. **Compounding Rewards**
   Delayed gratification allows you to benefit from the power of compounding. For instance:
   - Saving $500 a month at a 7% annual return grows to over $120,000 in 10 years.
   - Spending that $500 monthly on non-essentials results in no growth—and no marshmallows!
2. **Reduced Emotional Spending**
   Resisting impulsive purchases means more resources to allocate toward your goals.
3. **Strategic Investment Decisions**
   Delayed gratification equips you to withstand the psychological discomfort of market volatility, enabling you to hold investments through downturns and reap long-term gains.

Strategies to Build Delayed Gratification

1. Set Clear Financial Goals

- Define specific, measurable objectives:
    - *Short-term*: Save $5,000 for an emergency fund.
    - *Long-term*: Accumulate $1 million for retirement.
- Break goals into smaller milestones to maintain motivation.

2. Visualize Long-Term Benefits

- Imagine the rewards of waiting: a debt-free life, early retirement, or financial independence.
- Use tools like vision boards or future-self journaling to make long-term goals feel tangible.

3. Automate Financial Decisions

- Set up automatic transfers to savings or investment accounts.
- Automation removes the temptation to spend by making disciplined financial actions effortless.

4. Create a Reward System

- Celebrate small victories to reinforce the habit of waiting. For example:
    - Reaching a savings goal? Treat yourself to a modest indulgence.
    - Hit an investing milestone? Take a weekend trip.

5. Practice Gradual Delays

- Train yourself by incrementally increasing the time you wait for non-essential purchases. For example:
    - Want a new gadget? Wait one week before deciding.
    - Over time, extend the waiting period to one month.

6. Reframe Spending Temptations

- Instead of thinking, *"I'm depriving myself,"* shift to, *"I'm investing in my future."*
- This positive reframing helps align your actions with your long-term goals.

The Link Between Patience and Prosperity

Delayed gratification is not about deprivation; it's about prioritizing your future self over fleeting moments of indulgence. The ability to wait isn't just a financial strategy—it's a mindset that permeates every aspect of life.

Real-Life Example:

Consider two individuals:

- **Alex**: Spends every paycheck on immediate pleasures.
- **Taylor**: Allocates 20% of income to savings and investments.

After 20 years, Alex has little to show for their income, while Taylor has built a diversified investment portfolio, demonstrating how delayed gratification shapes financial destinies.

Key Takeaways

- **Delayed gratification is the cornerstone of wealth-building**, enabling you to prioritize long-term financial growth over short-term pleasure.
- The lessons from studies like the Marshmallow Test show that those who can wait often succeed in multiple areas of life, including finances.
- With clear goals, automation, and reframing, you can train yourself to delay gratification and unlock exponential growth in both wealth and personal fulfillment.

In the next chapter, we'll explore the emotional challenges that come with wealth-building, such as stress, comparison, and lifestyle inflation—and how to navigate them without compromising your financial goals.

Chapter 7: The Emotional Costs of Wealth

We often associate wealth with freedom and security, yet the pursuit and management of money come with significant emotional challenges. Stress, fear, guilt, and the pressure of comparison can undermine even the most diligent financial plans. This chapter explores the emotional side of money, the pitfalls of emotional spending and lifestyle inflation, and strategies to overcome FOMO (fear of missing out) while detaching your self-worth from material possessions.

The Hidden Emotional Costs of Wealth

Building wealth is not just a technical journey but an emotional one. Financial milestones—whether it's saving for retirement, buying a home, or achieving financial independence—often come with invisible baggage.

1. Stress

Money-related stress is one of the most common emotions tied to wealth.

- Fear of losing money, making poor decisions, or falling short of financial goals can keep you in a constant state of anxiety.
- Even wealthy individuals face stress, often in the form of managing investments, navigating taxes, or safeguarding assets.

2. Fear

Fear manifests as:

- *Fear of risk*: Avoiding investments that could grow wealth due to a fear of loss.
- *Fear of scarcity*: Worrying that you'll run out of money, even if you're financially secure.

3. Guilt

People often feel guilt when their financial success outpaces that of family or friends, leading to uncomfortable dynamics and self-imposed restrictions on enjoyment.

4. Comparison

In a world of social media, it's easy to compare your financial status to others.

- Seeing others buy expensive homes, cars, or vacations can create feelings of inadequacy.
- This "comparison trap" can lead to impulsive decisions aimed at keeping up with perceived standards.

Emotional Spending and Lifestyle Inflation

1. The Trap of Emotional Spending

Emotional spending occurs when we use money to cope with stress, boredom, or insecurity. Examples include:

- Buying expensive items to "reward" yourself after a tough week.
- Impulse shopping to boost mood or confidence.

While these purchases may offer short-term relief, they can derail long-term financial goals.

2. Lifestyle Inflation

As income increases, so do spending habits—a phenomenon known as lifestyle inflation.

- What starts as occasional splurges (e.g., dining out, upgrading gadgets) can quickly become normalized expenses.
- Over time, higher spending erodes savings and investments, making wealth-building more difficult.

3. The Underlying Cause: Emotional Triggers

Both emotional spending and lifestyle inflation are fueled by deep-seated emotional needs, such as the desire for validation, comfort, or belonging. Recognizing these triggers is the first step toward regaining control.

Overcoming FOMO and Detaching Self-Worth from Material Possessions

1. Understanding FOMO

Fear of missing out (FOMO) drives many poor financial decisions. Examples include:

- Joining in expensive group activities to avoid feeling left out.
- Investing in "hot" trends without research because others are doing it.

FOMO feeds into emotional spending and comparison, creating a vicious cycle of financial insecurity.

2. Shifting Your Mindset

To combat FOMO, reframe your perspective:

- Recognize that social media often highlights curated, exaggerated versions of reality.
- Focus on what truly aligns with your values and brings you joy, rather than chasing external validation.

3. Detaching Self-Worth from Material Possessions

In a consumer-driven culture, many people equate their value with what they own. This mindset leads to:

- Excessive spending on status symbols (e.g., luxury cars, designer brands).
- A constant feeling of "not enough," no matter how much wealth is accumulated.

To break free, practice the following:

- **Gratitude**: Focus on what you have rather than what you lack.
- **Minimalism**: Shift your priorities from owning more to living meaningfully.
- **Internal Validation**: Measure your success by personal growth, relationships, and purpose—not possessions.

Strategies to Navigate the Emotional Side of Money

1. Embrace Emotional Awareness

- Keep a journal to track emotions tied to financial decisions.
- Recognize patterns of stress, guilt, or comparison and address the underlying causes.

2. Set Emotional Boundaries

- Learn to say no to situations that pressure you into spending against your values.
- Avoid comparing your financial journey to others'—your goals and circumstances are unique.

3. Create a Value-Based Budget

- Align your spending with what truly matters to you (e.g., experiences, family, or education).
- Budget for joy: Set aside a small percentage for guilt-free indulgences to avoid the pendulum of over-restriction and splurging.

4. Practice Mindful Spending

- Pause before making non-essential purchases. Ask yourself: *"Does this align with my goals and values?"*
- Delay impulsive decisions by implementing a "cooling-off" period, such as 24 hours.

Key Takeaways

- Emotional costs like stress, fear, guilt, and comparison are an inevitable part of the wealth journey.
- Emotional spending and lifestyle inflation can undermine financial progress, but awareness and intentionality can help you stay on track.
- FOMO and materialism thrive on external validation—counter them by focusing on gratitude, values, and internal success.
- By managing the emotional side of money, you'll not only protect your financial goals but also cultivate a healthier, more fulfilling relationship with wealth.

In the next chapter, we'll delve into practical strategies for creating lasting financial habits that ensure your wealth-building efforts remain consistent and effective.

Chapter 8: Building Wealth Habits That Last

When it comes to building wealth, success isn't about grand, sweeping changes or one-time windfalls. Instead, it's about small, consistent actions repeated over time. At the heart of these actions lies the power of habits. Developing the right financial habits can transform your relationship with money, allowing you to build wealth effortlessly and sustainably.

In this chapter, we'll explore the psychology of habit formation, show how tiny but consistent actions compound into significant financial gains, and teach you how to create "default habits" that make good financial decisions automatic.

The Psychology of Habit Formation

Habits are automatic behaviors triggered by specific cues. According to Charles Duhigg's **Habit Loop**, every habit has three components:

1. **Cue**: The trigger that initiates the behavior (e.g., receiving your paycheck).
2. **Routine**: The action itself (e.g., transferring part of your paycheck to savings).
3. **Reward**: The benefit or satisfaction gained from the behavior (e.g., seeing your savings grow).

When repeated, this loop reinforces the habit, making it automatic over time. Building wealth through habits is about designing intentional loops that encourage smart financial behaviors.

Why Habits Matter in Wealth-Building

- **Automation Reduces Decision Fatigue**: Willpower is limited, and constantly deciding how to save, spend, or invest can be exhausting. Habits take decisions off your plate, ensuring consistency.
- **Small Wins Build Momentum**: Each small, successful action strengthens your confidence and motivation to continue.
- **Habits Compound Over Time**: Just as compound interest grows your money, habitual actions grow your wealth.

The Power of Small, Consistent Actions

Building wealth doesn't require large, dramatic efforts. It's about starting small and staying consistent.

1. The $10/Day Principle

Imagine saving or investing just $10 a day:

- At a 7% annual return, you'll have over $120,000 in 20 years.
- Starting small makes the process manageable and sustainable, especially for beginners.

2. Regular Investments

- *Example*: Dollar-cost averaging involves investing a fixed amount regularly, regardless of market conditions. This habit builds wealth steadily while minimizing emotional decisions.
- Over decades, even modest contributions grow into significant sums, thanks to the power of compounding.

3. Behavioral Compounding

Just as financial compounding multiplies money, **behavioral compounding** multiplies effort. For instance:

- Consistently sticking to a budget each month helps you identify and eliminate wasteful spending.
- Regularly tracking expenses leads to better decision-making over time.

Creating "Default Habits" for Wealth

The best habits are the ones you don't have to think about—they're built into your routines and systems. Here's how to create default habits that lead to financial success:

1. Automate Good Financial Decisions

Automation removes emotions and reduces the risk of forgetting or procrastinating. Examples include:

- **Automated Savings**: Set up a direct transfer to your savings or investment account the moment your paycheck arrives.
- **Debt Payments**: Automate loan or credit card payments to avoid late fees and reduce debt consistently.
- **Recurring Investments**: Schedule regular contributions to retirement or brokerage accounts.

2. Attach Habits to Existing Routines

Pair new financial habits with something you already do daily.

- *Example*: Every morning, check your account balances after reading the news. This keeps you mindful of your financial status.

- *Example*: Review your monthly budget at the same time you pay your bills.

3. Use Visual Cues

Make your financial goals visible to remind yourself of their importance.

- Create a progress chart for savings goals.
- Place a sticky note with your financial mantra (e.g., "Save for freedom, not for things") near your workspace.

4. Set SMART Goals

Effective habits start with clear, actionable goals. Ensure your financial objectives are:

- **Specific**: "Save $5,000 for an emergency fund."
- **Measurable**: Track progress weekly.
- **Achievable**: Start small, such as saving $100 per paycheck.
- **Relevant**: Align with long-term priorities, like financial security.
- **Time-bound**: Set deadlines to create urgency and focus.

5. Leverage Rewards to Reinforce Habits

Reward yourself when you hit milestones to make the process enjoyable.

- Example: After saving $1,000, treat yourself to a small luxury.
- Over time, the sense of accomplishment becomes its own reward, making the habit self-sustaining.

Overcoming Challenges in Habit Formation

1. Breaking Bad Habits

Identify habits that hinder your financial goals, such as:

- Impulse shopping.
- Relying on credit for discretionary expenses. Replace these with alternatives, like creating a wish list and waiting 30 days before purchasing.

2. Staying Consistent

- Track your habits daily to build accountability.
- Forgive setbacks. Missing one day doesn't mean failure; it's an opportunity to recommit.

3. Adapting Over Time

Financial goals evolve, and so should your habits. Regularly review and adjust your routines to match new priorities.

A Life Built on Wealth Habits

Wealth isn't built overnight, and it doesn't rely on extraordinary effort—it depends on small, consistent actions. When you create habits that prioritize savings, control spending, and encourage long-term investments, financial success becomes inevitable.

Key takeaways for building wealth habits:

1. **Start small**: Even $10 a day can lead to significant growth.
2. **Automate**: Let systems do the work for you, reducing effort and emotion.

3. **Celebrate progress**: Reward yourself to reinforce good habits.
4. **Be adaptable**: Update habits as your financial needs and goals evolve.

By mastering the psychology of habit formation and integrating these strategies into your life, you create a foundation for wealth that will last a lifetime. In the next chapter, we'll explore the long-term mindset necessary to think like the wealthy and stay focused on your ultimate financial goals.

Part 3: Solving the Wealth Equation – Aligning Math and Mind

Chapter 9: The Long-Term Mindset – Thinking Like the Wealthy

Wealth-building isn't just about earning more money or making smart investments—it's about adopting a mindset that supports sustainable growth over decades. Wealthy individuals think differently about time, risk, and money. They embrace the long-term mindset, focusing on goals that extend far beyond immediate rewards.

In this chapter, we'll explore how adopting this perspective can transform your financial journey. Using the RC Wealth Formula as a foundation, you'll learn to prioritize financial independence over instant gratification, think strategically about money, and align your actions with a vision for the future.

The Wealthy Mindset: How the Wealthy Think Differently

Wealthy individuals often share a distinct approach to time, risk, and money:

1. **Time**
    - Wealthy individuals view time as their greatest ally. They leverage the power of compound growth by starting early and remaining patient.
    - Instead of focusing on quick wins, they aim for strategies that yield consistent returns over the long term.
2. **Risk**
    - They understand that calculated risks are essential to growing wealth.

- While many fear losses, the wealthy see temporary setbacks as opportunities to learn, adjust, and grow stronger.
3. **Money**
    - To the wealthy, money is a tool, not a goal. They use it to create opportunities, freedom, and security, rather than simply accumulating it for its own sake.

Applying the RC Wealth Formula to the Long-Term Mindset

The **RC Wealth Formula**—$\text{Real Wealth} = \text{Material Wealth} \times (1 + \text{Mental Wealth Factor})$—perfectly encapsulates the importance of a long-term mindset.

How It Relates to Time, Risk, and Money:

- **Material Wealth** grows steadily over time through consistent saving, investing, and earning.
- **Mental Wealth Factor** reflects the patience, discipline, and mindset required to stay the course, even when faced with short-term setbacks or temptations.
- Together, these elements amplify Real Wealth, creating financial security and freedom that extends across generations.

The Role of Mental Wealth in Long-Term Thinking

Material Wealth without the right mindset is often fleeting. For example:

- Someone might inherit a fortune but squander it through impulsive decisions or short-term thinking.
- Conversely, someone with modest resources but a high Mental Wealth Factor can steadily grow their wealth over time.

Focusing on Long-Term Goals

Why Long-Term Goals Matter

Short-term wins, like buying a new car or earning a quick return on an investment, may bring momentary satisfaction. However, long-term goals provide lasting fulfillment and financial stability.

Examples of Long-Term Goals:

- Achieving financial independence.
- Building a retirement fund.
- Creating generational wealth for your family.

Wealthy individuals prioritize these goals because they understand that true wealth isn't measured by today's luxuries but by tomorrow's freedom and security.

How to Stay Focused on the Long Term

1. **Define Your "Why"**
    - Why do you want to build wealth? Is it to retire early, travel the world, or provide for your family?
    - A clear purpose keeps you motivated during challenging times.
2. **Track Progress, Not Perfection**
    - Break long-term goals into smaller milestones.

- Celebrate progress, even when it feels slow, to stay engaged and motivated.
3. **Resist Instant Gratification**
    - When faced with temptation, ask yourself: *"Will this purchase bring me closer to or further from my goals?"*
    - Reframe sacrifices as investments in your future self.

Reframing Your Mindset: From Instant Gratification to Financial Independence

One of the greatest shifts you can make is reframing how you think about time and money:

1. **See Time as an Asset**
    - Time is a compounding factor in wealth-building. The earlier you start saving and investing, the more exponential your growth.
    - Every dollar you save today grows exponentially over decades.
2. **Embrace Delayed Gratification**
    - Learn to trade today's pleasures for tomorrow's freedom.
    - Recognize that each decision to save, invest, or spend wisely is a step toward financial independence.
3. **Think in Terms of Value, Not Cost**
    - Instead of asking, *"How much does this cost?"* ask, *"What value does this bring to my life?"*
    - Align spending with your values and long-term goals.

Real-Life Applications of the Long-Term Mindset

Case Study 1: Early Investor

- **Scenario**: Alex starts investing $500/month at age 25, earning a 7% annual return. By age 65, they accumulate over $1.3 million.
- **Lesson**: Small, consistent actions taken early create massive long-term wealth.

Case Study 2: Short-Term Thinker

- **Scenario**: Taylor spends every paycheck on immediate desires, with little regard for saving or investing. At age 65, they have minimal savings and face financial insecurity.
- **Lesson**: A lack of long-term thinking often leads to stress and regret later in life.

Strategies to Cultivate a Long-Term Mindset

1. Visualize Your Future Self

- Imagine what financial independence looks like: What will you do? How will you feel?
- Use visualization to make your long-term goals tangible and motivating.

2. Adopt the "1% Rule"

- Focus on improving by just 1% every day, whether it's saving slightly more, reducing unnecessary expenses, or learning about investments.
- Over time, these incremental improvements lead to exponential growth.

3. Avoid Emotional Decisions

- Stay the course during market downturns by focusing on long-term trends rather than short-term fluctuations.
- Use automated systems for saving and investing to reduce emotional interference.

4. Surround Yourself with the Right Influences

- Engage with people, books, and resources that reinforce long-term thinking.
- Avoid environments that encourage impulsive spending or get-rich-quick schemes.

The Wealthy Think Long-Term—and So Can You

The RC Wealth Formula reminds us that Real Wealth is not just about the accumulation of Material Wealth but also about the mindset and habits that sustain it. By adopting a long-term perspective, you'll align your actions with your values, prioritize financial independence, and build wealth that lasts for generations.

Key takeaways for cultivating a long-term mindset:

1. Time, patience, and consistency are your greatest allies in wealth-building.
2. Reframe sacrifices today as investments in tomorrow's freedom.
3. Align your decisions with long-term goals, avoiding the trap of instant gratification.

In the next chapter, we'll delve into the power of consistency and incremental gains, showing how small steps can lead to massive progress over time. Let's continue building your roadmap to Real Wealth.

Chapter 10: The Power of Consistency and Incremental Gains

Building wealth is not a sprint; it's a marathon. The secret to long-term financial success lies in small, consistent efforts over time. These seemingly minor actions may feel insignificant at first, but they compound into extraordinary results, both mathematically and mentally.

In this chapter, we'll explore the immense power of consistency, introduce the "1% Rule," and explain how steady, incremental progress leads to sustainable wealth-building. You'll learn why avoiding the temptation of "big leaps" is crucial and how the RC Wealth Formula reinforces the value of consistent actions.

The Role of Consistency in Wealth-Building

Consistency is the bedrock of financial growth. Whether it's saving a portion of your income, investing regularly, or sticking to a budget, small actions repeated over time deliver exponential results.

Why Consistency Works

1. **Leverages Time**: Time is your most powerful ally in wealth-building. Consistency allows you to harness the full potential of compounding.
2. **Reinforces Good Habits**: Regular practice builds discipline and aligns your financial behavior with long-term goals.
3. **Minimizes Emotional Interference**: Consistent actions, like automated savings or investing, reduce the influence of emotions during financial decisions.

The "1% Rule": Tiny Improvements with Massive Results

The "1% Rule" is a simple yet transformative principle: Focus on improving by just 1% every day. While 1% may seem trivial, its impact grows exponentially over time, thanks to the power of compounding.

The Math of 1% Improvements

Let's consider the math:

- If you improve by 1% daily, you'll be **37 times better** after a year, as the gains compound: $(1.01)^{365} \approx 37.78$

The same principle applies to wealth. Incremental improvements in saving, spending, or investing—such as increasing your savings rate by 1% each month—can lead to monumental progress over time.

The Mindset of 1% Gains

Mentally, the 1% Rule keeps you motivated by breaking large goals into manageable steps. Instead of feeling overwhelmed, you build momentum through small wins that accumulate into lasting success.

Avoiding the Trap of "Big Leaps"

Many people fall into the trap of chasing big, dramatic changes in their quest for wealth. While bold moves might yield short-term results, they're rarely sustainable and often come with significant risks.

The Risks of "Big Leaps"

1. **Emotional Burnout**: Drastic changes can feel unsustainable, leading to frustration and giving up.
2. **Increased Risk**: High-stakes decisions, like speculative investments, may result in significant losses.
3. **Overlooking Fundamentals**: The pursuit of quick wins often distracts from foundational habits like saving, budgeting, and consistent investing.

The Alternative: Steady, Sustainable Growth

Wealth-building isn't about making a single groundbreaking decision. It's about stacking small, smart choices over time. Sustainable growth ensures stability, reduces risk, and builds a foundation for long-term success.

Applying the RC Wealth Formula to Consistency

The **RC Wealth Formula**—Real Wealth = Material Wealth × (1 + Mental Wealth Factor)—highlights the importance of consistent action.

How Consistency Impacts the Formula:

1. **Material Wealth**: Regular saving and investing steadily grow your financial resources.
2. **Mental Wealth Factor**: Consistency reinforces discipline, patience, and emotional intelligence, increasing your Mental Wealth Factor over time.
3. **Real Wealth**: Together, these small, consistent actions compound, amplifying your overall wealth and security.

Strategies for Building Consistency

1. Start Small and Scale Up

- Begin with manageable steps, such as saving 5% of your income.
- Gradually increase your efforts, like raising your savings rate by 1% each month or year.

2. Automate Your Finances

- Automate savings, debt repayments, and investments to ensure consistency without requiring daily decisions.
- Automation reduces the risk of skipping contributions due to forgetfulness or emotional interference.

3. Track Progress and Celebrate Wins

- Use tools like spreadsheets or budgeting apps to monitor your financial growth.
- Celebrate small milestones, such as hitting your first $1,000 in savings or completing a year of consistent investing.

4. Focus on Long-Term Goals

- Align your daily actions with your vision for the future.
- Revisit your financial goals regularly to stay motivated and course-correct if needed.

5. Embrace the Power of Routine

- Embed financial habits into your daily life. For example:

- Review your budget every Sunday.
  - Invest a set amount on the 1st of every month.

Real-Life Examples of Incremental Gains

Case Study 1: The Steady Saver

- **Scenario**: Maria saves $300/month starting at age 25, earning 7% annual returns. By age 65, she accumulates over $380,000.
- **Lesson**: Small, consistent contributions over time lead to significant growth.

Case Study 2: The Big Leaper

- **Scenario**: James waits until age 40 to invest, then contributes $1,000/month. Despite larger contributions, he only accumulates $300,000 by age 65.
- **Lesson**: Starting early with smaller amounts often outperforms later, larger contributions.

Consistency: The Bridge Between Math and Mind

Consistency isn't just about repeating actions—it's about creating a synergy between the **math** (financial strategies) and the **mind** (habits and mindset).

Key takeaways for consistency:

- **It's not about perfection**: Small missteps don't derail your progress; consistency over time smooths them out.

- **Patience is key**: The greatest results often take years or decades to materialize, but the wait is worth it.
- **Focus on the process**: Success lies in the daily effort, not in waiting for a single big breakthrough.

Final Thoughts

Wealth-building is a journey of persistence, not perfection. The power of small, consistent actions—guided by the principles of the RC Wealth Formula—ensures that every step you take moves you closer to Real Wealth.

As you continue this journey, remember: incremental gains might feel slow, but their impact compounds into extraordinary results. In the next chapter, we'll redefine financial freedom and explore how to align your wealth with your values to create a life that's truly fulfilling.

Chapter 11: Financial Freedom Redefined

For many people, the term "financial freedom" conjures up images of luxury: mansions, expensive cars, lavish vacations, and a bank account that never runs dry. But this idea of freedom often comes with its own chains—a relentless pursuit of "more" that can leave us feeling unfulfilled, overwhelmed, and disconnected from what truly matters.

True financial freedom isn't about how much money you have—it's about having enough money to live life on your own terms. It's the ability to align your financial decisions with your values, passions, and purpose, so you can spend your time and energy in ways that bring meaning and joy.

In this chapter, we'll explore what it really means to be financially free, the concept of "enough," and how to align your financial goals with the life you truly want to live.

Redefining Financial Freedom

At its core, financial freedom is about **choice**. It's about creating a life where you're not controlled by money—whether that means living paycheck to paycheck or endlessly chasing more wealth.

Financial Freedom Is:

- **Security**: Knowing you have enough money to cover your needs and unexpected challenges.
- **Flexibility**: Having the financial resources to make choices that align with your goals and values.
- **Time**: The ability to prioritize what matters most—whether that's family, health, creativity, or

exploration—without being tethered to work out of necessity.

Financial Freedom Is Not:

- About achieving a specific number in your bank account.
- Defined by society's expectations or comparisons to others.
- A one-size-fits-all destination—it's deeply personal and unique to you.

True financial freedom begins when you take control of your finances and redefine success based on what matters most to *you*.

The Concept of "Enough"

One of the greatest traps in the pursuit of financial freedom is the idea that *more* is always better—more income, more investments, more possessions. This mindset often leads to a cycle of endless striving, where no amount of money feels like it's enough.

What Does "Enough" Mean?

"Enough" means having the financial resources to:

- Meet your basic needs (food, shelter, healthcare).
- Support your desired lifestyle and priorities.
- Feel secure in the face of uncertainty or emergencies.

It's the point where your money supports your well-being and values without driving you into stress or overwork.

The Pitfalls of Chasing More

- **Burnout**: Working endlessly to earn more can leave little time for relationships, health, or personal growth.
- **Diminishing Returns**: Research shows that after a certain point, additional income has little impact on happiness. Studies in psychology suggest that emotional well-being plateaus once basic financial needs are met.
- **Comparison Culture**: The pursuit of "more" is often fueled by societal pressure and the need to keep up with others, leading to dissatisfaction even when you're financially comfortable.

The key to avoiding these pitfalls is learning to recognize and embrace *your* definition of enough.

How to Find Your "Enough"

1. **Define Your Priorities**: What truly matters to you? Is it time with family, creative freedom, travel, or giving back to your community?
2. **Set Financial Goals Based on Values**: Instead of chasing an arbitrary number, align your goals with your priorities. For example:
   - "I want to save enough to take a year off and travel."
   - "I want to retire early to spend more time with my children."
3. **Avoid Lifestyle Inflation**: As your income grows, resist the urge to constantly upgrade your lifestyle. Focus on building security and freedom, not possessions.

When you embrace "enough," you free yourself from the pressure of constantly needing more. Instead, you can focus on enjoying the wealth and opportunities you already have.

Aligning Financial Goals with Values and Purpose

True financial freedom comes when your financial goals reflect who you are and what you want to contribute to the world. It's about using money as a tool to support your values, passions, and life purpose—not as the end goal.

Step 1: Reflect on Your Values

Ask yourself:

- What do I value most in life? (e.g., family, creativity, freedom, personal growth, helping others).
- Does my current financial behavior reflect these values?

For example, if you value adventure, are you saving for meaningful experiences like travel? If you value creativity, are you allocating resources to pursue a passion project?

Step 2: Identify Your Life Purpose

Your financial goals should align with your broader sense of purpose. Consider:

- What impact do I want to have on the world?
- What legacy do I want to leave behind?
- How can my money help me live a life that feels meaningful and authentic?

Your life purpose doesn't have to be grand or world-changing—it might simply mean living in alignment with your values, caring for your loved ones, or pursuing your dreams unapologetically.

Step 3: Set Purpose-Driven Goals

Once you've identified your values and purpose, create specific financial goals to support them. For example:

- If your purpose is to spend more time with family, you might aim to pay off debt so you can work fewer hours.
- If your passion is helping others, you might set aside a portion of your income for charitable giving.

When your financial goals are tied to your values, money becomes a means of empowerment, not a source of stress.

A New Definition of Success

Redefining financial freedom also means redefining success. Instead of measuring success by how much you earn or accumulate, consider these questions:

- Am I living in alignment with my values?
- Do I have the freedom to spend time on what matters most to me?
- Am I able to make choices without being driven by financial fear?

By these standards, financial freedom isn't a finish line or a number in your bank account—it's a state of being. It's the feeling of security, flexibility, and fulfillment that comes when your money supports the life you want to live.

The Ripple Effect of Financial Freedom

When you achieve financial freedom, it doesn't just benefit you—it creates a ripple effect in your family, community, and beyond. Here's how:

- **For Your Family**: Financial freedom allows you to be present with your loved ones and provide security for future generations.
- **For Your Community**: With financial flexibility, you can give back, support causes you care about, or mentor others on their own wealth journey.
- **For Yourself**: By aligning your finances with your purpose, you create a life that feels rich in every sense of the word.

Key Takeaways

1. **True financial freedom isn't about having more money—it's about having enough to live life on your own terms.**
2. **The concept of "enough" helps you avoid the endless pursuit of wealth and focus on what truly matters.**
3. **Aligning your financial goals with your values and purpose creates a life of meaning and fulfillment.**
4. **Redefine success as the ability to live authentically, choose freely, and spend time on what brings you joy.**

As you reflect on your journey through this book, remember: the ultimate goal of the wealth equation is not just to build material wealth, but to create a life of balance, freedom, and purpose. Your real wealth is measured not by how much you have, but by how well you use it to live a life that feels true to who you are.

You've redefined financial freedom—now it's time to live it.

Conclusion: Mastering the Wealth Equation

Throughout this journey, we've explored the intricate dance between the math and the mind behind money. We've examined how numbers—income, expenses, savings, and investments—form the foundation of wealth, while the intangible forces of psychology—patience, discipline, mindset, and emotional intelligence—amplify its impact. Together, they complete the **Wealth Equation**:

$$\text{Real Wealth} = \text{Material Wealth} \times (1 + \text{Mental Wealth Factor})$$

This formula is more than just a mathematical representation; it's a philosophy that bridges the tangible and intangible aspects of wealth-building.

Balancing the Math and the Mind

We've delved into the importance of balancing these two sides of the equation. Financial success doesn't come from understanding every formula or chasing every investment trend. Instead, it's about making deliberate, consistent choices that align with your values and goals.

- **The Math**: Provides structure, helping you track, calculate, and optimize your financial decisions.
- **The Mind**: Fuels the discipline, resilience, and clarity needed to stay the course and avoid being derailed by emotions or short-term temptations.

Together, they form a holistic approach to wealth that is sustainable and fulfilling.

Financial Success is About Alignment

Mastering the Wealth Equation isn't about perfection—it's about alignment. When your actions reflect your priorities and your mindset supports your goals, every step you take moves you closer to financial freedom.

What Alignment Looks Like:

- You save and invest not out of obligation but out of commitment to your future self.
- You spend money intentionally, knowing it aligns with your values and brings joy or utility.
- You view challenges—market downturns, unexpected expenses—as opportunities to adapt and grow, rather than insurmountable obstacles.

Approaching Your Finances with Confidence

You now have the tools to master both sides of the equation:

- The analytical skills to manage your finances effectively.
- The emotional intelligence to navigate the psychological challenges of wealth-building.

With clarity in your numbers and confidence in your mindset, you can approach your financial journey with purpose and resilience.

The Final Word: Wealth is More Than Numbers

Ultimately, wealth isn't just about money—it's about what money allows you to do. It's about freedom, security, and the ability to live life on your terms.

"The wealth equation isn't just numbers—it's the sum of your actions, habits, and mindset. Master both, and you'll not only build wealth but also the life you've always wanted."

As you close this book and step into your financial journey, remember: small, consistent actions guided by clear values and a strong mindset will lead you to not only financial success but also a meaningful and fulfilling life.

Appendix and Bonus Material

This section is designed to provide you with practical tools, exercises, and resources to help you apply the concepts from this book and continue your journey toward financial freedom. Whether you're looking for budgeting templates, mindset exercises, or further reading, you'll find everything you need here to stay on track and achieve your financial goals.

Appendix 1: Quick Reference Financial Tools

1. Sample Budget Templates

These simple templates can help you take control of your finances by organizing your income, expenses, and savings.

The 50/30/20 Budget Template

Category	Percentage	Monthly Amount	Notes
Needs (Essentials)	50%		Housing, utilities, etc.
Wants (Discretionary)	30%		Entertainment, hobbies
Savings/Investments	20%		Emergency fund, retirement savings

- Example: If your monthly income is $4,000, allocate $2,000 to Needs, $1,200 to Wants, and $800 to Savings/Investments.

Zero-Based Budget Template

Income	Expenses	Amount
	Rent/Mortgage	
	Groceries	
	Transportation	
	Entertainment	
	Debt Repayment	
	Savings/Investments	
	Miscellaneous	
Total Income - Total Expenses = $0		

- This template helps ensure every dollar is accounted for and aligned with your financial goals.

2. Compound Interest Calculator

Use this quick formula to calculate how your investments can grow over time:

Future Value (FV) = P(1 + r/n)^(nt)

Where:

- **P** = Principal amount (initial investment)
- **r** = Annual interest rate (in decimal form, e.g., 0.06 for 6%)
- **n** = Number of compounding periods per year
- **t** = Time in years

Example

If you invest $10,000 at a 7% annual return, compounded annually, for 20 years:

- FV = $10,000(1 + 0.07/1)^(1×20) = $38,696.85

Online Tools

For simplicity, you can use free online calculators like:

- Investor.gov Compound Interest Calculator
- Bankrate's compound interest calculator.

3. Investment Tracking Spreadsheet

Keep track of your investments to monitor your portfolio's growth, diversification, and performance:

Date	Investment Name	Asset Class	Amount Invested	Current Value	% Gain/Loss	Notes
01/01/2024	ABC Mutual Fund	Stocks	$5,000	$5,500	+10%	Long-term holding
03/01/2024	XYZ Bond Fund	Bonds	$3,000	$3,100	+3.33%	Low-risk asset
04/01/2024	Real Estate REIT	Real Estate	$2,000	$2,200	+10%	Diversification

You can create and customize a spreadsheet in Excel or Google Sheets to fit your portfolio.

Appendix 2: Wealth Mindset Exercises

1. Journaling Prompts to Reframe Money Beliefs

Use these prompts to explore and challenge your current money mindset:

1. What beliefs about money did I learn growing up? Are they helping or hindering me now?
2. What's one financial fear I have, and where does it come from?
3. How do I define financial success, and does that definition align with my values?
4. What would financial freedom look and feel like in my life?
5. If money were no longer a source of stress, how would my life change?

2. Visualization Exercise for Long-Term Goals

This exercise will help you connect emotionally with your financial goals:

Step 1: Imagine Your Future Self

Close your eyes and visualize your life 10, 20, or 30 years from now. Picture yourself financially free:

- Where do you live?
- How do you spend your days?
- Who are you with?
- What goals have you accomplished?

Step 2: Write It Down

Describe this vision in vivid detail. Be specific—this makes the goal feel more tangible. For example:

- "I live in a cozy home by the beach, working part-time on passion projects. I'm debt-free and travel twice a year with my family. My investments provide steady income."

Step 3: Break It Into Steps

What financial actions do you need to take to make this vision a reality? Write down three steps you can start today.

3. Habit-Tracking Templates

Use a simple tracker to reinforce positive financial habits:

Habit	Daily	Weekly	Monthly	Goal	Progress
Save $100/month			Yes	$1,200/year	
Track all expenses	Yes			Build awareness	
Invest $200/month			Yes	$2,400/year	
Read a personal finance book		Yes		6 books/year	

Print this template or use a digital habit tracker to stay consistent.

Appendix 3: Recommended Reading and Resources

Here's a curated list of books, podcasts, and tools to deepen your understanding of financial literacy and behavioral finance:

Books

1. **"The Psychology of Money" by Morgan Housel**
   Explores how emotions and behavior influence financial decisions more than math.
2. **"I Will Teach You to Be Rich" by Ramit Sethi**
   A practical, actionable guide to managing money, saving, and investing.
3. **"Your Money or Your Life" by Vicki Robin**
   Focuses on redefining your relationship with money and aligning finances with life purpose.
4. **"Rich Dad Poor Dad" by Robert Kiyosaki**
   A classic on financial education and understanding how to build wealth.

Podcasts

1. **"Afford Anything" with Paula Pant**
   Focuses on achieving financial independence and living intentionally.
2. **"The Dave Ramsey Show"**
   Offers practical advice on budgeting, paying off debt, and financial planning.
3. **"ChooseFI" (Choose Financial Independence)**
   A podcast dedicated to financial independence strategies and early retirement.

Online Tools

1. **YNAB (You Need A Budget)**
   A budgeting app that helps you allocate every dollar and stay on track.
2. **Mint**
   Free financial tracking app for budgeting, goal-setting, and managing debt.
3. **Personal Capital**
   Great for tracking your net worth, investments, and retirement progress.

Appendix 4: The RC Wealth Equation – Bridging Material and Mental Wealth

In this appendix, we'll revisit one of the most powerful concepts introduced in this book: the **RC Wealth Equation**, which highlights the essential balance between the tangible (material wealth) and intangible (mental wealth) aspects of financial success. This equation offers a simple yet profound framework for understanding how math and mindset work together to create real wealth.

The RC Wealth Equation

Real Wealth = Material Wealth × (1 + Mental Wealth Factor)

This equation bridges the gap between the **math of money** and the **mindset of money**, showing that true financial success requires more than just accumulating material resources—it also depends on how you think, feel, and behave with your money.

Breaking Down the Equation

1. Material Wealth

This represents the tangible, measurable side of wealth:

- Your **income**: The money you earn through work, investments, or other sources.
- Your **savings**: The money you've set aside for future needs or emergencies.
- Your **investments**: Assets like stocks, bonds, real estate, or businesses that grow your wealth over time.

- Your **assets**: Property, vehicles, or other items of value that you own.

Material wealth is the foundation of financial success, but it is only one piece of the puzzle. On its own, material wealth does not guarantee security, fulfillment, or freedom.

2. Mental Wealth Factor

The *Mental Wealth Factor* is a multiplier that reflects your psychological alignment with money. It includes:

- **Discipline**: The ability to stick to a budget, invest consistently, and avoid impulsive spending.
- **Patience**: The willingness to delay gratification and let wealth grow over time.
- **Emotional Intelligence**: Managing emotions like fear and greed that often lead to poor financial decisions.
- **Mindset**: Your beliefs and attitudes about money, such as whether you operate from a mindset of scarcity or abundance.

A low Mental Wealth Factor (e.g., lack of discipline, emotional spending, or fear-driven decision-making) can diminish the impact of even substantial material wealth. On the other hand, a high Mental Wealth Factor can amplify the value of more modest material wealth.

What the Equation Teaches Us

The RC Wealth Equation reveals that **real wealth** isn't just about the numbers—it's about how effectively you use your material wealth to create a fulfilling life.

Key Implications of the Equation

1. **Material Wealth Alone Is Not Enough**
   Even if you have significant income, savings, or investments, a low Mental Wealth Factor (e.g., poor habits, unmanaged emotions) can limit your real wealth. For example, someone with high earnings but unchecked emotional spending may feel financially unstable despite their material resources.
2. **Mental Wealth Can Amplify Modest Material Wealth**
   Even if you have moderate material wealth, a high Mental Wealth Factor can significantly enhance your financial outcomes. Strong habits, patience, and an abundance mindset can help you stretch your resources, make smarter decisions, and achieve greater satisfaction with less.
3. **The Balance Is Essential**
   The best results come when both material wealth and mental wealth are strong. By focusing on improving your Mental Wealth Factor while growing your material wealth, you unlock the full potential of your financial resources.

Illustrative Scenarios

Scenario 1: High Material Wealth, Low Mental Wealth

- **Material Wealth**: $1,000,000
- **Mental Wealth Factor**: 0.2 (poor financial habits, fear-driven decisions)
- **Real Wealth**: $1,000,000 × (1 + 0.2) = **$1,200,000**

In this scenario, the individual has substantial material wealth, but their poor mental alignment (e.g., emotional spending, lack of patience) limits how effectively they can use their resources. They might experience stress, instability, or dissatisfaction despite their high income and assets.

Scenario 2: Moderate Material Wealth, High Mental Wealth

- **Material Wealth**: $500,000
- **Mental Wealth Factor**: 1.0 (strong habits, patience, and discipline)
- **Real Wealth**: $500,000 × (1 + 1.0) = **$1,000,000**

In this scenario, the individual's mental wealth doubles the value of their material wealth. Their strong habits (e.g., consistent saving and investing, avoiding emotional decisions) allow them to maximize the utility and security of their financial resources, leading to a sense of stability and freedom.

How to Increase Your Mental Wealth Factor

Improving your Mental Wealth Factor doesn't happen overnight, but consistent effort in the following areas can create significant progress:

1. **Develop Discipline**
   - Automate savings and investments to remove temptation and ensure consistency.
   - Stick to a realistic budget aligned with your values.
2. **Practice Patience**
   - Embrace long-term thinking in investing and wealth-building.
   - Resist impulsive decisions driven by short-term emotions.
3. **Enhance Emotional Intelligence**

- Learn to manage fear during market downturns and avoid greed during bull markets.
- Reflect before making financial decisions, especially big ones.

4. **Adopt a Growth Mindset**
   - View financial challenges as opportunities to learn and grow.
   - Replace limiting beliefs ("I'll never have enough") with empowering ones ("I can create opportunities to grow wealth").

The Synergy of Math and Mindset

The RC Wealth Equation shows us that financial success isn't just about accumulating material wealth—it's about creating a balance between the math and the mindset. By improving your Mental Wealth Factor, you can:

- Stretch your financial resources further.
- Make better decisions that align with your values and goals.
- Experience a greater sense of security, freedom, and fulfillment.

Whether you're just starting your wealth-building journey or have already achieved significant material success, this equation is a reminder that the mind is as important as the math.

Practical Steps to Apply the RC Wealth Equation

1. **Evaluate Your Material Wealth**
   - Assess your income, savings, investments, and other assets.

        - Identify areas where you can improve, such as increasing your savings rate or diversifying your portfolio.
2. **Reflect on Your Mental Wealth Factor**
        - Be honest about your financial habits, mindset, and emotional responses to money.
        - Use the journaling prompts from Appendix 2 to uncover and reframe limiting beliefs.
3. **Set Balanced Goals**
        - Combine material goals (e.g., "Save $10,000 this year") with mental goals (e.g., "Develop the discipline to stick to my budget").
        - Focus on both improving your finances and strengthening your mindset.

Final Note: Unlocking Real Wealth

Your wealth is more than just the sum of your assets—it's a reflection of how effectively you use those assets to create a meaningful and fulfilling life. The tools, exercises, and resources provided in this book are here to support you as you continue your journey toward financial freedom.

The RC Wealth Equation reminds us that true wealth isn't just about accumulating material resources—it's about balancing the math of money with the mindset behind it. By consistently strengthening both your Material Wealth and your Mental Wealth Factor, you can create not just financial success, but a life aligned with your values, passions, and purpose.

Remember: building wealth is a marathon, not a sprint. The real magic happens when math meets mindset—when you combine sound financial principles with patience, discipline, and emotional intelligence. By bridging the gap between material and mental wealth, you unlock your full financial potential and create lasting wealth in every sense of the word.

Your wealth-building journey is just beginning—take the next step, make it your own, and watch how your financial success amplifies your ability to live the life you've always envisioned.

www.ingramcontent.com/pod-product-compliance
Lightning Source LLC
Chambersburg PA
CBHW071034240526
45469CB00006BD/2211